TRIBE

First published in 2008 by
The Dedalus Press
13 Moyclare Road
Baldoyle
Dublin 13
Ireland

www.dedaluspress.com

ISBN 978 1 904556 89 3 (bound)
ISBN 978 1 904556 77 0 (paper)

Dedalus Press titles are represented in North America
by Syracuse University Press, Inc., 621 Skytop Road,
Suite 110, Syracuse, New York 13244, and in the UK by
Central Books, 99 Wallis Road, London E9 5LN

Typesetting and Design: Pat Boran
Cover image © Hadleigh Thompson

The Dedalus Press receives financial assistance from
An Chomhairle Ealaíon / The Arts Council, Ireland

TRIBE

Mary Montague

DEDALUS PRESS
DUBLIN, IRELAND

ACKNOWLEDGEMENTS

The author wishes to express her thanks to the editors of the following publications in which a number of these poems originally appeared:

ANTHOLOGIES: *Beyond the Rubicon* (Covehill Press, 1999), *Brass on Bronze* (Errigal Press, 2005), *Breaking the Skin* (Black Mountain Press, 2002), *Eleven Ways to Kiss the Ground* (Errigal Writers, 2001) and *A North West Christmas Anthology* (Yes Publications, 2004). JOURNALS: *The Black Mountain Review, Crannog, Cyphers, Exile, www.thelondoner.com, Poetry Ireland Review, The SHOp* and *west47online.*

Grateful thanks are due to the Arts Council of Northern Ireland for an award under the 2002 Support for the Individual Artist Scheme.

Thanks also to the Tyrone Guthrie Centre at Annaghmakerrig, Co. Monaghan, for time spent there.

I would also like to thank the following: the Errigal Writers for their support and close reading; Denise Blake and Imelda Maguire; Joan and Kate Newmann; John Montague and Elizabeth Wassell.

To Ann Breslin

Contents

TRIBE

*"All earthly living things are certainly descended
from a single ancestor."*
—Richard Dawkins,
River out of Eden: A Darwinian View of Life

*"[T]he great Tree of Life ... fills with its dead
and broken branches the crust of the earth,
and covers the surface with its ever branching
and beautiful ramifications."*
—Charles Darwin,
On the Origin of Species by Means of Natural Selection

A Voice in the Wilderness

As a child I wept
that animals had no souls.

The legends of evolution
lent me joyous righteousness

but my father argued with me
and I floundered

under the lash
of his acerbity.

At night, after the Rosary,
I read until sated:

gorging on dinosaurs;
murmuring the soft music of the ages—

Cambrian; Silurian; Devonian;
Carboniferous; Permian; Triassic.

I hissed Ordovician sibilants,
told myself Cretaceous tales,

of individuals indescribable
with flesh and blood, horns and teeth.

The Lioness and the Oryx

It is said
that on God's holy mountain
there shall be no hurt, no harm;
the wolf shall dwell with the lamb,
the leopard lie down with the kid,
the calf and the lion together.

Any number of fables
strain with the same sentiment;
how the creatures of the forest,
the fauna of the savannah,
the browsers of leaves, the devourers of flesh,
dwell in harmony,
each with the other.

The body craves it.
The soul sings it.
The mind goes back
to the small child
that Isaiah said would lead
lamb, wolf
leopard, kid
lion, calf
and back to another
who buried her first kitten
killed by a savaging dog,
buried that sweet softness
among the blushing pansies in the rockery;
buried
and wept.

We grow up.
We learn to accept.

My cat today
is innocent as any child,
innocent as the finches, the sparrows,
the shrews, the fieldmice,
she brings home
to banter with, abandon,
unskinned, half-eaten.

She watches
while I sweep
each little carcase into the dustpan.

It is reported
that in Africa,
on the arid plain of Samburu,
a lonely lioness
treads a hopeless patrol
accompanied by the oryx calf
she has adopted.

The child in me, vigil-keeper
at the rockery,
rejoices.

But Earth is not Heaven
and cannot suffer
this disturbing solicitude.
Only in the human mind
are we unfettered
from inexorable immovable governance
by cycles, rhythms, laws,

which bind
all voices in the wilderness.

The lioness is deranged;
the oryx calf is doomed.

A New Foal

Diffusing
for years into an ether;

spreading thin,
becoming substanceless;

drifting
into some mild lagoon;

swimming briefly
in coral light;

then making landfall—
a desert shore.

Trudging eternal terraces of sand;
coming finally to a thorny plain;

building a rough cottage
from discarded blocks of stone—

harsh and comfortless,
but yours.

Ahead, an endless vista:
scrub and sand;

beautiful, even so,
in its raw wiriness of survival.

All day you grubbed
for food, dug for water,

guarded your empty cottage
in case it would be taken;

but in dawn's flare, in evening's
distillation, you stole moments.

You stared and stared

at one thing one tree one stone

one grain of sand.

You observed great dust storms
that raged across the prairie of your mind;

then you turned away.

And slowly words came:
in rosarial sequence,
paying out a meditation
on a single image;
or in a wash
that any fabric of sense
was too fragile to contain.

And look:
here they stand,
shaky as a new foal
on the pale blades of spring;
a creature changing
while you watch. Head
raised, ears pert,
soon ready
to canter off to deeper meadows.

Anatomy of the Horse

What made George Stubbs decide to make
the horse his subject? To choose a creature
of utility and show it worthy of the same
respect as any classical god or ideal form?
A focus on horseflesh so consummate, paint
so animate, the story goes that Whistlejacket himself
reared up at his own image. After years
as a jobbing portraitist, when he came to his modest
inheritance, the man left wife, children, his familiar
trade, for this madness: to hole up in a Lincolnshire
barn with carcases now dignified as 'horse cadavers';
to slowly strip layers of flesh to its bone. Months
on each corpse. Years in total. A decade distilled
to *The Anatomy of the Horse in Eighteen Tables*
all done from Nature. It is *A particular Description*
of the Bones, Cartilages, Muscles, Fascias, Ligaments,
Nerves, Arteries, Veins and Glands that omits
the gore, rot, stench, flies, the risk of disease,
to yield—chalked, pencilled, inked, etched–
clean dissected glory. What does it say, this intemperate
looking, this practised *knowing* of an animal
from the marrow out? That earnest laborious
devotion to detail, worship of the gritty factual,
is love. George Stubbs loved horses;
not lightly, easily, sentimentally;
but brutally, culpably, viscerally,
unashamedly; heart, blood and sinew.
And every touch of paint betrays
the depths he would reach to,
the heights transcended.

Unveiled

after George Stubbs and Robin Blake

The dun-coloured surface receding to backdrop
is, like the wall of a cave, the bare stage
for stark conformations of ochre and henna.

Brood mares, a classical frieze, as on a Grecian urn;
except that flesh breathes off the canvas; the poses
are wholly absent of artifice. Movement sweeps,

undulates, through the still bodies on their poised
struts, summer coats contouring their figures closely
as skin: a slung torso, its dip of spine; the swell

of rump and belly; slope of withers; swoop of throat;
how a face slants from a tangled fall of mane; the loose
fray of tail. It is as though purdah were lifted. Here

equine nudes in all their female grace make
a conversation piece of the communal domestic:
mothers, gravid or suckled; the matrons, the virginal;

and, of course, children, as yet undefined, with heads
shaded into their dams' flanks, and tails like rags of felt.
A grown filly eavesdrops distractedly on exchanges

of eye-contact, ear-angle. One blowsy chestnut,
near her time, turns to stare over her shoulder, a gaze
pregnant with query. A nursing madonna umbers

into brooding reverie. Each study has the glow
of an individual animal but the gathering makes
a tableau of familial rapport through bodies

naked of landscape, context or language: stark
conformations of chestnut and bay on a dun-
coloured surface that recedes into backdrop.

Hambletonian, Rubbing Down

A sequence after George Stubbs

1.

The bay stallion, big as himself, is offered
on Newmarket's table—a polder-like landscape
defeated by a weight of sky, its distance furlonged
by three plain buildings sailing to the horizon.

The familiar rubbing-down house, refuge
and comfort after the toils of victory, is
at a good remove, stage-right, a childish
building with shuttered eye askance, abashed.

Across an aeon of space, the winning post stand
presides over a suture of rail that notches
the heath's leanness like a push of faint
spine through the cling of taut flesh.

2. The Artist's Monologue

This could be the last time. I will get it right. I know my own worth.

A strange feeling, to return to Newmarket. A homecoming, of sorts. Some settlement; reshaping.

I can only know this animal in silence.

A creature not made to reflect glory on us!

'Paint him at his victory'. His victory. Which feels to him like abuse.

The narrative of the horse-race, which must not be recorded in its beforeness; only in the afterwards, history secured, we can look and say there is how it happened. Victory replete. The garlanded hero at his reward.

I said to Vane-Tempest (oh, the felicitousness of the appellation!): Sir! I cannot supply you with victory in isolation. I know my Art, Sir. I know my subject. I cannot simply please the mob. I am an Artist, Sir. You must depend on my Artistry. Form. Balance. Symmetry. Above all, Truth. From Nature, Truth.

You know it yourself, Sir. The public do not want just the roar of victory, the press of the crowd, the chaos of the finish. They want to know the hero. They want some part of him. There are those who follow the jockey, swarm to the bright of his silk; those who slap the back of the trainer; those who tribute the owner, partake of his toast; but most want the horse; the horse that draws their phaeton of dreams; the animus *of possibility, their fancy of glory.*

The only means are by privacy: privacy and silence.

The particular of the thoroughbred: the equine sublime; noble, generous, the balanced perfection of power and elegance.

I won. He wanted only the winning post. I insisted also on the rubbing-down house. He demanded one work, the time-shift of 'Gimcrack'. I replied that I am not that man of four decades since. Has not my artistry advanced over my lifetime? Do we stick to the fashions of the mid-century? No. I will have Hambletonian, rubbing down, and I will have him on his own canvas.

The crowd can wait. I know my own worth.

They have relegated me as a mere animalier. Even Wedgwood's company astonished that I could portray a human face with accuracy. It is a poor fact that a new excellence is viewed as narrowness, exclusiveness, rather than refinement. There is not a man in England, nay, in any realm, that can paint a horse half as well as me; and they think that this expertise can fashion just a single creature! Well. No matter. Horseflesh is my exegesis, my nemesis.

Hambletonian. You will also be my subverted victory.

Finally. The canvas. Larger than I have sought for quite some time. But it is not far from me. The Beacon course, its lofty stands, its bank, the filament of rail.

Fix the horizon. Stake the buildings.

Victory as a horse at full stretch.

The horse is stretched.

A stroke. A skim. This is all I need.

The reach of head. The strain of neck. The long surrender of torso. A shadow of mastoido-humeralis. The flank's scoop of obliquus externus.

The creature is not in repose. Clench of hock. Brace of knee. Flex of pastern. Weight—off centre. Off balance. Gallop implicit in his agitation.

There must be disturbance.

Teeth, grimaced like a death mask.

Spare the flanks. Just a smear of foam at the bit. Don't overdo it.

But the eye. A bewildered pained eye.

3. Riposte

What do you say, sir, through the body of this creature? Indeed,
these creatures! Why would I pay three hundred guineas to be insulted?
Was it for this I lost hours of sleep? Where is the victory,
the triumph, the adulation? Nothing but my fearful-looking horse
and my glowering servants. Of course the horse is beautifully done.
The whole country knows your expertise, Master Stubbs;
but one would think that when granted a commission, a painter
might bear in mind the sensitivities of his patron. I risked
for that horse. The victory came as sore to me as to him.
If this is your reflection on all that investment, the time, money,
training, feeding, hiring and firing, boasting and challenging,
then to hell with you man! It's no wonder your reputation
is sinking when you do so little to mend it! You may fight me
through the courts if you dare. With luck, you won't live
to see the end of it. How would you have my horse?
Roaming a wilderness? He wouldn't last a day! And those men
have no opinions! It is not for them to comment on how I treat
my property. They forget themselves, as do you. You are all
in my hire, all in my keeping. I will not pay for this outrage!
If your sympathies are so much with my horse, Master Stubbs,
keep him to doat on yourself!

4.

The artist got better with age, gathering himself,
like his subject, for a final magisterial effort;
all craft's refinements filtered by a lifetime's
observation and empathy. The yield is bas-reliefed
from Newmarket's muted palette; dominates
the canvas; dwarfs the mulish handlers.

Animal cartography; the sacramental body
in the shape of a horse. Your gaze caresses
like a lover's: voluptuous musculature pressed
against thin integument; smooth delineation
of gaskin, stifle, brisket; the slightest
corrugation of ribcage; bald weep of chestnut.

If a fly landed, the flesh would shiver.

The horse has too much presence. Step back. Take a breath.

The pale sky is late afternoon, late spring;
mild, fresh as linen. The hinterland lopes away.

Then – you're fixed by the handlers' stare,
the lad's pause, the trainer's switch of attention:
an undertow of accusal; as if, voyeur,
you've caught the horse naked.

You have caught the horse naked.

How beauty blinds, disguises its distress.

This is Christ at Newmarket, martyred on the desert heath.

The Word

after John the apostle

In the beginning was the word
and the word was in the code
and the word was the code.
It was in the code in the beginning.
Through the code all life came to be.
Not one life had its being but through the code.
All that came to be had flesh through it
and that flesh was the joy of creatures:
mortal flesh, built out of chaos;
inventive flesh, that death can't extinguish.

The code was the first word
animating all flesh
that came into the world.
Flesh grew from the code,
had its being through it,
but flesh knew only itself.
Then, through mutation of the code,
consciousness arose out of flesh
and language could celebrate
this fresh power.

Where it is manifest
flesh bears witness
to a different way of being in the universe
through the power of the word
born not out of instinct
or sexual urge
or any dictate of the code

but out of word alone.
Word was made flesh,
dwells inside us.
We glory in it:
the glory of us, fruits of evolution,
creatures of conscious awareness.

Indeed, from this fullness we have, as a species,
received truth in return for awareness
since, though the word was first given through the code,
knowledge and truth have come through the flesh.
We cannot fathom the word,
but flesh evolving from the code
has made it ours.

Umbilicus

Days
when it felt
like it would throttle me
like a noose.

Days
when I fought its lasso
as desperately
as a feral horse.

Once free
I thought I would run forever
my feet bruised and throbbing
from the roughness
of the ground between us.

Days
I thought you were lost
to me as I was
to you.

Now
little can repair
the damage done.

Our house
will not be restored
but still
we live in it.

Between us
stretches that silver cord
shining as when it held us
bound
in the amniotic lair.

To My Mother

I've just bought it, my own birthday present
from you; the first one, harbinger of a new
era, not good but inevitable. The years
of the frivolous, the desperate clanging
attempts to lure me to your notions
of femininity, are over. Times,
I felt like your changeling, that you
thought me foreign as Siberia. Now
I'd take the gilt glamour, your chunky
jewellery and horrendous fashions.
Anything to show that you'd left
the gritty detritus of your bed, gone browsing
in cheap boutiques and bargain basements,
forgotten your pain for an afternoon.
So, today, with your birthday money,
I found myself at the jewellers, settling
for earrings you'd never have bought for me:
small studs with a Celtic spiral, silver
to your gold, modest to your flamboyance.
If you could've chosen these for me.
If you could've gifted our difference.

To the Registrar of the General Medical Council, London

I write in response to your recent letter
to my father. It is with (*strangely burning*)
regret that I must inform you that he
has been diagnosed (*this time last year*)
as suffering from dementia.

He's been demented for longer:
chess moves in the patterns of tiles;
bridge ploys his constant conversation
with me who never learned to play.
He stares from the cave of his duvet
with a hunted look; talks of winter
rations, troop movements—battening
to hoard survival's crumbs.

I presume this circumstance
means that his registration
is no longer tenable.

He watches me:
the same furtive surveillance
with which I eyed him
as a child—disinterest as decoy;
but keeps the clear blue chill
of his gaze true to the fault
lines, the shifts that could mean
the sea ice opening.

Nevertheless
I would like to inquire
if it is possible for him
to retain his title.

It is the thing he is proudest of:
achieved aged twenty-three.
Sixty years is a long downhill.
All the same, I can see it was a beacon
clawed towards from the slums
of Brooklyn, the bogs of Tyrone,
as the lit fuse of his intelligence
hissed through cellars
of poverty, disappointment.

His intelligence. Now it sputters,
crackles in odd corners, sparking
through a mess of confusion, rage
and fear. It's still spoken of
with something like reverence in this parish,
his old practice, where he arrived
as a fresh scion of the newly-minted
National Health Service and was greeted
by a mixture of suspicion and awe:
a Catholic doctor? Whoever heard
of such a thing? He was twenty-eight, most eligible,
but despite his periods in Dublin, Whitehaven,
Kent, was raw and pious as a cleric.
He tended that practice like a shepherd,
losing himself in service, inspired
by a simmer of fractured confidence
and clouded empathy to a dedication
approaching love. The startling acquisition,
in his forties, of wife, children, brought no ease;

only more anxiety, which he shouldered,
sidelined, in the name
of his all-encompassing duty.

When I was young, his standing in the community
was a scald to me who knew him
differently. Now it is some slight comfort
when yet another in a long line
of ex-patients tells me, voice
grave with appreciation,
that he was a great doctor.

Over twenty years after leaving home
I have some glimmer
of the forces, the imperatives,
that drove him.

They are not a stone's throw from my own.

So. While the doctor may be demented
he is still the doctor—in the fifties, only a breath
from the priest and from God.

My father was a committed public servant
who managed a single-handed practice
for almost forty years. Being a doctor
was everything to him. I trust that *(at least for now)*
he can remain, technically, a member
of the medical profession. With thanks

Sincerely

his daughter.

Labyrinth

It was already there
before I came to the scene.
I had no hand in its making
yet I was the one assigned
to hold the torch aloft
and lead the way out.
The builders were tired
and wanted to do no more
than sit and admire
the ghostly patterns
thrown by leaping flames
onto the limed walls.

I was young and fawning
and wanted to do good.
So I sat for a time and listened
to their hallowed stories,
their foundered hopes,
their clutching dreams.
I heard much to make me weep,
to mourn and pity. Because
I was young, and with a certain
animal strength, I could coax
them a little way through the labyrinth.
I would sometimes rush ahead
through several chambers
thinking I saw a light, but
when I turned for them
they seemed to be in a different
place and, more, the path
ahead had shifted. I could
no longer trace its way.

Progress, they ruled, was null
and void, and they, who had previously
seemed hewn from the rock itself,
now suddenly burned molten,
geysered, at my effrontery.

But that cold confusing place
dampened everything; so
I kept on trying. Gradually
the intricacies wove their own
tortured spell. Each foray for air
became shorter, the air itself
was danker, and the tunnel's
lumen was closing in, its ceiling
crumbling into my scalp.
I no longer spared energy
for my companions. I could hardly
see them anyway in the dark
and when I called them, they
laughed at me, sneering
at my efforts to escape. I couldn't
shake them off. They hovered,
gloating—I'd sometimes glimpse
their raging eyes in an odd flash
of reflected light. A faint smell of freshness
was all I trusted; trying to source it
took me on a deadening perambulation
without even scratching the surface,
just getting deeper and deeper
into this hollow tomb. I'd feel
strangely free for days, but then
the awful loneliness would collapse
me again and I'd struggle back
to be further stunned by their

indifference. I was still weeping
but now for myself. I knew
I couldn't live like this,
couldn't breathe this choking space,
no matter what they'd settled for.

It happened that I was no longer
young and, it seemed, no further
forward. Wraithing despair condensed
and threatened to choke me. Yet
somehow every difficult step,
each blind search, all confused
pursuit, had built incrementally
into some kind of perplexed wisdom
that matched the furrows of my brain:
I knew this place; I knew them and,
unbelievably, I knew myself. All
that was left was beyond, and beyond
I didn't know but I knew how to reach it.
So I went and it was as simple
and powerful as that. Terrible too.
My own blood is left on the walls
to guide them out if they'll only
lift one of those dying torches
to see it. They could still make it
but increasingly their chances diminish.
They remain, shrouded with dust
and ashes, calcifying in ammonite
halls. One day I'll go back
to mark their fossilised entrails.

There comes a time

There comes a time when mourning has to cease:
ashes, heaped in the grate, are an avalanche
waiting its blowdown. Time
to sweep them up, take them out.
It is safe. They have cooled.
To keep faith with bereavement
is to deny the possibility
of movement. Still, to leave now
feels like betrayal of the long
nightwatches. So you wait.
You study the ashes: variegated,
like grey tabbies, a vague litter
piled up. Shapeless as old griefs.
If you reach your hand the dull
plush gives through: fleshless,
formless, nothing to rub against.
Already hollow, even as you tried
to stave off absence; but real enough
to coat the whole room;
to choke any new kindling.

Leaving My Father's House

This is the last time I am going in:
my only chance in this darkness
with no-one else to see. The dim porch
is almost reassuring, a sanctum
with magazine racks and collection tables
pushed against the wall. Familiar
objects of routine and ritual. I dip
one hand in the font; with the other
I twist the smooth, slightly battered
knob of the inner door, pull
it to me. The space inside is vast
yet cluttered. Cold moonbeams slant
from high arched windows. Suspended
between defiance and paralysis,
I lift my hand to my lips, suck
holy water from my dripping fingertips.
The taste is cool, slightly stale, metallic.
I have tasted better. I go in.

Everything looks different in darkness
but the eyes adjust. Shades of grey
accumulate, shadow themselves into form.
On golden days when this cavern
was walled with light and colour I feasted
on the bread of angels, felt glimmerings
dissolve on my tongue. In these pews
I studied holy writ. At the rails
I closed my eyes, parted my lips.
At this altar I bared my throat.
In a humid confessional, I begged.
I have knelt, I have prayed, I have whispered
This is my body. This is my blood.

The hot sore blister of the true presence
gutters at me. Oh how I fixed on that light,
looked for it in the smooth bland faces.
Sometimes in my darkness I felt
the softest glow diffuse from an embered
centre; but there was no lasting heat.
Now I see it for a tawdry trinket,
a tiny bulb behind coloured glass.
I can no longer afford to believe in it.
The flame is not real. They have buried
the talent. I feel all the old clichés
rise in me: compassion, forgiveness
and the like. I will let them go. I have
granited myself against the chill
of this cold palace. Not even a mother's
mildness can intercede for me now.

I turn from the altar, face a long aisle.
This place is so different at night. The stained
glass is dull as a bruise. The holy pictures
are ghoulish. I am sick of the sanctification
of suffering, the clutch of pieties. I must
leave this place of memory and marble,
walk out alone and in darkness.
Through the frozen strobe of moonlight
I begin. My heels strike a bald rhythm
into the hollow air. I get to the door,
reach for the tablet of brass and pause.
I taste my own salt and I am not afraid.
I will take my last look. Briefly, briefly
for there is nothing to keep me.

I push through to the porch where
footsound shrinks and flattens. My breathing
is a soft tear in the quiet. There is no
peace yet, just the energy of decision.
I came back for my father's blessing
and found only strangeness. I cannot
live in a porch. I must find a new
dwelling place. I must learn
new ways to bless myself.

Sperrins

Driving home, they summon me from the Foyle
Bridge. They disappear for the long dip but,
as I crest the Glenshane Road, they surge languidly,
tawned, mellowed, by inundations of sun.
They're like the graph of ovarian hormones
during the oestrus cycle: there's Sawel
in the first phase, climbing to the highest
peak; then Dart, almost matching it
in the second part of the cycle. Coursing
on from them, varying swathes that banner
the skyline. I lose them at the turn-off
for Claudy but on the descent to the village,
they crowd up, an undulating herd
arching, fading, to the haze of horizon,
flowing on into Tyrone. Together
they make a bevy of reclining nudes,
smooth-hipped and shouldered; a pod
of birthing seals piled up on each other,
sleek, sensuous, as a Henry Moore.
On Learmount Road, Sawel looms
with the conformation of a great recumbent
mare, the bluff of the summit, her withers,
the crease in her flank marking the curve
of her body, its sheltering belly.

Shadow

There's a horse loose in Learmount forest.
I've seen it myself, a tree-shadowed flash
of bay or dun or grey; and I've heard it—
both of us heard it in that steep-sided ravine
that runs down from the road, its staves of trees,
clumps of rhododendron, the trail a precarious
sill—*there;* a snort, muffled thump of hooves
on the soft path. Neither of us said anything
what with the rush of our breathing, our bodies'
rustle against brambles and leaves as we heaved
up the steep climb; and there was little chance
catching it, all those trees, no clear ground;
but the hoofprints—surely they'd never
been there before? Girls keep their ponies
to the main trails—hardly ever ride Learmount.
You never saw tracks here—the narrow path,
its overhanging branches, precipitous
fall—a rider couldn't stay on. And so many,
so fresh: lean sickles printing each other,
notching the span where long cantering strides
gave out, where feet hit the ground. Taut
with alertness we thudded on, hushing our breath
to listen. Where the trees halted, tracks dissolved,
sponged on the clearing's tussocks; and *horse*
was dispelled on our broken-winded gasps.

Now when I walk there, the slant of branch
has the slope of withers, a stand of bushes
breaks the bulk of rump, and everywhere
a forelock-straggled eye gleams from a tangle
of foliage. If I spin at a blackbird's cackle,
I glimpse the swing of darkness cantering off;
then a wren darts from a clump or a magpie
shouts its outrage, and when I look again
the movement is gone. It must have been caught
by now, but the thought of its freedom spices
my rambles, the tracks still numerous, though
fading, overmarked by bootprints. Still, a horse
could be lucky, keep to the thickets in daylight,
there's enough rough grazing in the thistled
clearings to content a hardy animal. Given
a drizzle of goodwill, a seed of brains and caution,
it could get by for years. So I'll keep on searching
for my dryad, tarpan—my shadow of yearning.

Sunlit Morning

A sunlit September morning. Bright balsam-light
planing through poles of Sitka spruce,
ambering under a honeycombed canopy
to tan the leaflitter, its shag of needles,
shale of beech. Now a sound, soft shush
like finest rain, a light spray through the trees;
but there is no rain, no wind. I look up
through the rough furze of spruce
to see a definite motion, a purposeful
swing. The cause imprints momentarily
against pale yellow glare as it scuttles
along a branch: a lithe weasel-like
body with a brush of tail that's thinned
by the combing of light. It headlongs
up the trunk, then trapezes across
to the next tree and is followed
by another, then another. The trees'
pine-green plumage swishes and sweeps
as three red squirrels make a vertical
slalom to ford the air. I curdle with pleasure:
a remnant of ancient fauna survives
in a hybrid plantation. The lead squirrel
descends to the floor, glances back:
pixie head, monocular gaze
holding me briefly as its forelegs
splay beyond the hunch of back,
the feather of tail. I flick for the others
and when I look again the squirrel is gone.
They are all gone. The woods are silent.

Sperrins Autumn

1. Autumn Dress

Sheltered by a host of pine,
like costumed children
against the dark green,
the coppiced beeches,
trimmed to bouffant plumpness,
introduce the new season
with a lamé of rust.

2. Forest Fire

Air has the pared-downness, the bone,
of autumn; light has the slant of winter's
stealth. Walking uphill, the path cuts a deep
furrow through this mixed plantation,

massed ranks of beech with sinuous grey
bodies cordoned by taller Scots pine
whose stiff poised forms interlace ruffs
of greenery along their branches' wrists.

It's been dry and soft of wind these last
few weeks. A plenitude of turned leaf
arrays the beeches. Yet they are generous:
the ground is silted with their castings,

an almost molten layer that resolves
as thin curled flakes of copper and bronze
which crunch and sigh underfoot. The foliage,
the dry furnace for this spillage, fuelled

by a burst of late afternoon's bleary
sun, now blazes to a conflagration
of auburn and rust. The wind stirs
and a few sparks drift slowly down.

3. Amethyst Deceivers

Think of ballgowns of muted plush
or the gatheredness of long-sleeved
peasant blouses: crinoline; brushed
cotton; crêpe. Their stems have the fragile
elegance of a bare-shouldered neck.
Their caps radiate with nuances
of lilac and mauve. Damp velvet.
We are deceived in not expecting
them but they are too dignified
to surprise, too gentle to startle;
the pleasure of colour's discretion,
its emancipation in the flesh.

4. Stain

Autumn sprinkles the woods with spice, and trees
cast for the privilege. This is the price
of divestment: the chestnut, profligate
with lemon and jasmine; beech, steeped in a glaze
of paprika, turmeric—a richness of savour
next to oak's dry coriander and cumin;
mustard of sycamore; pine's fresh bay leaf;
and bracken, faded to ginger and sage.
Berries of rowan lend a dash of chilli,
and, where a tea-dark mulch dresses the paths,
throngs of willowherb wave fronds of cinnamon.
The silk of leaf is squandered with spendthrift
flourish on the feast of fall, riot
of original stain seeping slowly through.

Winter Canvas

Bleak, bleak midwinter. Air pared to iron.
Monochrome of snow with Lowry-thin trees.
Chill of an empty mind. Enter the courtyard,
a blank quadrangle, clean-hemmed duvet
of white that dampens disquiet to frigid peace.

All spare, still. But there, a small shiver, a slight
undulating chestnut sinuousness.
The mind hesitates, casts for the name. Tongue
rushes to claim it, *stoat,* a fierce glottal thrust,
rich as blood, too weighty for this grace note
of creature that purls an aerial path over snow.

The pertness as it stops, rears, peers above
the crystal quilt. A direct stare, the black
globules of eyes like heads of two hatpins
embedded in foxy velvet. It dives again,
leaps, fluid staccato to swim a frosted
ocean. At the wall's cliff, it vanishes.

Left on the snow's linen: faint stitches of feet,
scuffs of belly; the palest remnant
of that muscular ribbon, that red flare.

Haunted

I follow a February snowfall
to Learmount's bedraggled terrain:
the forest—planted; the mountains—
stripped, barren as tundra. The wind
borrows the voice of a wolf
haunting his old range: *mac tíre,*
the country boy, that rascal, blackguard,
swaggerer, rustler, sheepstealer,
conniver and trickster. For all that
he is gone now. All his savvy
couldn't save him. Do the ravens

watching me from their church of Scots pine
miss him? The days as spearhead, rearguard,
the feasting on his gluttings must
crowd their folk memory. They
were the hunt's black druids, gloating
shadows of the bloodlet, motes
in the stunned glazing eyes of the dying.
Their ragged capes of wingspans still float
over the Sperrins to scan the landscape
for the blot of a carcase, but they reel
with a fatalism, black flags
suspended over an absence.

If I stop, stare back, these vigilants
will rise up, coughing their anger
so I walk on, sneaking them glances:
their thin tassel of beard feathers;
the blunt heavy bills; their cocked heads,
suspicious, watchful; how they have

hunched, making their backs echo
a rough sickle. Angels without their god,
devils without a furnace, they muster
as vagrants, relics in a paltrified world.

The heron

rises from the river at the sight of me,
undoing its seedy rakishness,
its poised presence in the water:

the sword of bill, up-pointed
with the tilt of alarmed head;
the yellow fish-shallow eye.

It floats off, blankets of wings
in slow-motion embrace
and release of air,

follows the river, lifts
above the trees, lurches,
swings around behind me,

head pulled back like the bolt
of a crossbow; legs trailing,
feet upturned like bulbous mittens.

Against the grey sky
a pterodactyl would not look
more surreal and primitive.

Winter Meditation

A dipper slicks from the stream's cobbled surface.
I pause at its beacon of breast bobbing
above water-smoothed stone. I could smile:
obsequious-seeming bows; the desperate
suavity of plump dapperness that wears
a white bib over mocha plush; but there's
nothing comical about this—roundness
is the bulk of downfeathers meshing air
into their underbrush; the staccato flash,
a blinked warning that throws the dipper
into relief against the stream's chiaroscuro—
the gleam and dark of stone-stuttered flow.

The bird whisks upstream, a burrish missile
deadlining the water, wings a-whir like lateral
rotaries. It vanishes with the river's curve.
My mind pursues, plunges, to where sluggish
prey, buffered in their amniotic lair, fatten
below terra firma's lean season. Into this chilled
suspension the marauder bursts; tosses
shallow cairns sheltering the likes of *ancylus*
or the infant larvae of stonefly, mayfly. The current
smooths bird-brownness to silky grey, pressing
from plumage an aura of bubbles that swathe
the sleek alien, then bead to the surface.

After a frenetic sweep the dipper will follow
its shining train back to the frigid scourge above;
shake off wetness, refluff feathers to swaddle
its slim form. Cold has settled on my own
oven of flesh, tautens the skin of my face,

clouds my breath, tingles ears, nose; numbs
hands, feet. I ponder the body's creep
out of water, the achieving of thermal
stability to thwart the vice of climate;
its price of constant stoking; this irony,
to return to forage unfrozen nourishment;
the cost of freedom in hunger and motion.

Owenkillew

Consider the cries as you stave up a last
Sitka-gloomed ridge: two notes, whingeing, pealing.
At the top, rest briefly to let breath settle, sweat
cool. Attend. Then enter the light. Drop down

to a rough lane that leads to a scruffy clearing,
willowherbed, meadowsweeted, where the shadow
of the trees' cliff finally releases. The view pans
to the Owenkillew valley, haunched by the sun-steeped

Sperrins, tweed, roan, ripening to olive and amber.
Stop. Be a bleb on the trail's contour line, arrested
by the picturesque, the story-book prettiness:
quilting of fields, appliqué of forest, the white rose

of the village below. Breathe deep, feel flesh
lighten, sun on your shoulders, the whole of the glen
at your feet. Now let the cries spear you. Look:
two buzzards soaring, unmistakable silhouettes,

the heavy glide on broad wings, their angled hinge
making of the body a taut sling, disarmed only
by the absence of a target for telescopic eyes.
Watch them climb towards the sun, an older

fluenter Icarus and Daedalus, swaying
on the ladder of updraft that banks
off Moneycarn. The pleas of Daedalus
chase Icarus higher. The two slew, yaw,

lurch to keep height, flashing pale tatters
of undercovert. They vanish into the sky's
eye, sucked up into glare. The voice of Daedalus
is a purgatorial echo; then, miraculously, this time

they both return intact: Icarus, half-crouched, plunging
behind the conifers of the far ridge; Daedalus's long skim
leaving only sporadic cries to sharpen the air,
original fierceness that leavens the tranquil.

Let attention liquefy, diffuse out
into the bowl of the valley. Light refracts
back to its colours, acquires the tone of substance.
Sperrinlands have shown their mettle: agrarian

rhythms and certitude, powerful domestic
reassurance, are edged with wildness. Now feral
yourself, scavenger of liminal strips of wilderness,
blissed by witness and by the predatory sun,

you may lope downhill to a named world of rows
and ways, lines and walls, but on your passage
through the antechamber of a hawed and hazeled
ravine, you will scatter sheep like a prophet.

The Squire

In Learmount, where the trail bends back
from the Faughan, I veered off down
a path rutted by a tractor's adderbacked
tyre-prints; skirted the vault of pines, skulked
into an overhang of rhododendron,
passing the rusted hulk of the old
water-wheel whose huge cogs indented
the air with frozen precision. The only
movement was from the gully beneath
where a tributary rushed to its confluence.
I tracked this noise, cramponing the valley's
rump, creeping through colonnades
of etiolated trees: birch, beech, ash;
all slendered by the stretch for sunlight.

Climbing the curve that led to the road,
I met the sauntering squire: a big dog-fox.
At the sight of me, his face puckered.
Almost lazily, disgustedly, he spun
and flung himself up the rise, his long
body a smear of coffee and cinnamon
against the faded crackling that remained
from the wood's autumnal undressing.
I lurched to a run, scrambling up the hill,
hoping for another glimpse. Of course
he was gone, dissolved into an April
afternoon: earth; leaflitter; bark; sunlight.

The Rooks' Return

In cold-season dusk
they are an explosion of homecoming.
The starved arms
of the bare trees are stretched
to reach them.
The leaf litter
is spattered with their uric graffiti.

You stand there,
a small tree yourself,
as condensing twilight
flattens, blurs, the surrounding shapes
and the sky drains
to a chilled darkness-blue.

You hear, at first, a distant chuckle,
a lapping tide, that amplifies, approaches
as a rasping corvid chorus. You see them,
as you've seen them other evenings from the hill
above the woods, like a black river, like a splay
flowing inwards and downwards to converge
on this hub of the forest, the belly in which you stand.

And they come carping, having seized their day
and now full of rough talk about it. As the witching
capes of their wings pell-mell over the treetops,
they shout their arrival, their right of way
with harsh masculine laughter, and you,
caught in their boisterous commuter confusion,
surge at their streeling vortex. They drop
so the trees, tufted, become hotch-potch

candelabra. The tufts holler
to familiar strangers, jostle and squawk
to take possession of a favourite roost
and settle in for the night,
drunk on each other's presence,
raucous with tales of the day:
warmth that sustains
until dawn.

Swallows

They hurl themselves above an acre of lawn
overlooking a tree-fringed lake. A paradise
of insects inspires them. They've lobbed
their fragile bodies over African swamp,
savannah, Saharan vastness, funnelled
into Europe through the Strait of Gibraltar
and flung themselves across to Ireland for this
aerial plankton. They're quick and agile
as their tiny prey: same darts, direction
changes, that give fly-swatting its tension.
They make it a gambol, their frenzied
metabolism fuelled by the flesh of thousands.
They dip, dive, swoop, loop, swarm
together, reel away, flatten out over
the blades, float up, circle and climb, then
peel off with a flash of sailor-white belly.
Every twist is a gauze of flickering wing;
each smooth-shouldered downstroke a surge
of orbital power, almost gravity-free
in a dart-like form that skims into long
shallow undulations. In sun, they iridesce
with indigo; in shade, they're swart as plum.
Blurred with speed, the fused pellet of head
and torso bisects a sickle of wing; only
time slows them enough to catch the tail's
lovely fork, the studs of white decorating
the membrane of its fan. They shark the air,
a dark unruly shoal, voices zipping staccato,
or, now, an unruly chirrip. Grown youngsters
buzz their parents across the grass
and they all rise, chittering, in a vertical dance,

its pinnacle an agape of bill, an insectivorous
kiss. Then they slide down the tent of air
and swerve off. Together, wings and tail
make a double pair, seen when they swing
their rumps forward, give a butterfly-flutter
to slow, to stall, to half-hover over some coarse
flower, transmuting their silhouette
to that Gabriel descended.

Avalon

1

Days oscillating between St Vincent's and Trepassy
in fog thicker than treacle; wondering, marvelling,
that Earhart ever took off. The capelin were late; the whales,
absent. The beach was a moraine of gravel and ash.
St Vincent's again. In the car park, a US RV, shut

as a summer house on a winter Wednesday. We trudged
the boardwalk as air, sky, sea, dissolved to a mesh
of moisture that beaded our hair, seeped into our clothes.
Smell of an Irish November, but this was July.
At the pavilion a teenager, with skin page-white

as our own, surveyed the emptiness: a summer job
to monitor tourists and we were awesome, real Irish;
her boyfriend would buy us a drink if he knew. *Newfie.*
She clamed the label like a badge of survival; then nodded
to the RV: *National Geographic photographer.*

A snort. *He's waiting for a shot of a whale with a fish
in its mouth. There's no capelin. No whales without them.*
We tightened lips, shook our heads, as if we didn't know,
hadn't planned for just this season of leviathans
thrusting onto the beach in pursuit. Conspiracy leaned

her closer. *When that thing pulled into this community—*
the term noosed lean littoral settlements—*it hadn't passed
Walsh's gas station when the phones started. They beat it
to the shore: 'Did you see what just pulled in?'* She laughed.
All the men came out of the pub. As she glanced away

her expression set like a lake's surface after wind dies. *Have you
tasted cod?* Mirth threatened to scramble my face. I avoided
your eyes. Then hers filled. *We love the cod,* she declared
passionately. I rushed to empathise: the moratorium,
quotas, selling off of fishing rights, collapse of stocks.

She stared. *You mean people in Ireland know about this?
They care about us?* How could I tell her? This was the hour
of the Tiger, Ireland gorging a brief flourish of wealth.
We'd no stomach for reminders of the years of lack
and of loss. You distracted her with talk of her future:

off to college, to Canada, in the fall. *Mom says I'll come back.
That I'll miss the whales. She did.*—Aren't you impressed by them?
She shrugged.—*I grew up with them. They're here all the time,
every summer.* We gazed out at the sea's slough as it rasped
the heaped cinders of the beach. There were no whales for us.

2

We consoled ourselves with the thought of Mistaken
Point, its Precambrian fossils; that flesh could indent
rock. (Things were so bad that spineless extinct microfauna
promised worthwhile viewing. Well, at least they were fixed.)
Backed by maps, directions, we set off into formless dank,

crawling at fifteen or less, sight being almost redundant
but for its constant alarm at the mouths of potholes.
Near-misses were exhausting; hits were jarring; and all
the while our wraithing shroud taunted with creeping
withdrawal ahead, closure behind, and sporadic

flinches that might yield the briefest licks of the Barrens.
Our eyes ached by the time we reached the dirt track.
Then, startling as if it leaped from the fog, a parked
SUV. Must be close. It was surely a record
of life. We climbed out to a faint pocked trail, noting slight

markers that could confirm the way back. The ocean hushed
us with its massing sibilance. Complaints of seabird
grew more vociferous. At the edge, slabby cliffs
slicked into fume. I retreated. Fears were timeless here.
A pirate's galleon could slide out of the haar.

We gave up on fossils. The thick haze stopped us fleeing
but we tracked ourselves back to the car with tightrope
concentration. The return drive was near-relief. Our dismal
report provoked the motel-owner to a satisfied
Nobody ever finds them. Card games passed the afternoon.

In the evening we braved a walk in Trepassy. Not just
a sunless, but a skyless summer. We were swimming
in a white-out of murk. How did they stand it? Young people
hung round the village hall, stiff, bored, but said *hello*
like good country children. No doubt they wondered

what the hell we were doing there. We took this wondering
to heart. Over a week and the fog wasn't for shifting.
Our retinas stung from staring it down. The motel
was a stalag, dull with winterlight; and the whales—
they were old rumour, false sirens, an idler's fantasy.

The Barrens

We fled the coast, determined to breach the fog,
clear Avalon, get to the west. As we hit
the main highway, the road straightened, smoothed
and slowly lengthened as mist was combed
to sparseness and finally lifted, burning
off with a filmy new sun. The world
had shed its damp swaddling; the stanching
of sight was over. Our focus could run
to a far horizon, eye muscles stretch and loosen
beyond hermetic vision. Free at last. The car,
curbed since the ferry, charged like a filly,
accretions of second gear blowing off
into the vast bowl of the Barrens. The Barrens,
rich to our gaze: a winter-green scrubland
of arctic fierceness; an ocean-huge heath roiled
by swathes of dwarf shrubs, laurel, juniper,
hunched with stubbornness; the serrations
of tuckamore—spruce, fir, reduced almost
to bonsai; all of it and the bleak stare
of peat-dark tarns, confirmed us in silence.

The road that bisected like a hairline crack,
undeviating, let both of us swish eyes
over the craggy undulations. This land
would never be cultivated, with bone
of it breaking the acid scalp of its soil.
Life was crouched with survival, but now, fresh
out of vapour, all was profusion and brightness;
a thick green sea below a blue of benevolence;
yet ours was the only movement except
for a single red kite that swooped, tacked,

specked. Of the great herds that the space invited,
there were none. Wilderness empty as Eden
after the Fall; scenery unlivened. As the road
threaded unremitting miles, the thrill cooled.
Details changed. The canvas didn't. Then
even detail blurred. We were aliens incast
to the maw of some great organism. The thin
solvents of civilisation—gas, rubber, tar—
were all we had to hold a course.
I remembered something about the Alps,
how it wasn't until the eighteenth century
they were commonly seen as beautiful.
Now I believed it. No beauty
without security. I clung
to the pattern of map in my head.

Encounter

The car crested a gradual rise and down
the long slope of its lea we saw a female
caribou, her whole bearing a checkmate.
As we coasted the decline, she held, broadside,
her panel of torso and haunch like the bulk
of drawing room furniture, its skilful finish of long
tapering legs making a delightful grace
to set the piece at a daringly high centre
of gravity. Her imperious neck; the open skance
of her ears; and her coat that was a hybrid
of season: summer-brown cape; winter-smoke
belly, throat, face; dark swatches from eye
to black nose. That close. Then she turned,
ran. We followed. She showed herself deer fitting
a wasteland: not one for bounding and leaping,
but animal to cover distance with her camel-like
stride, a slung trot, the back unexcited. Her hocks
swooped rhythmically, her fetlocks gave, sprang,
as shovels of hooves slapped the road's surface.

What happened next is not original, but
it doesn't lose in the telling: a story of mutual
gaze, two animals looking across the flatland
of their curiosity. The caribou slewed into the bush.
I stopped the car and got out. She'd already
halted in a shallow arena, waited for me
in a clearing of lichen and shale. To meet her,
I waded slowly through a furze of thigh-high
trees. We were not equal: I had history
to contend her with; she, antlerless, possibly
a mere year old, had only herself and trust

in the magic of her body to spirit her
from danger. Of course I wanted to touch her;
of course I knew she'd never let me; but I walked
on, singing, like a low desperate unconvincing
siren: *Pretty girl, baby, don't be afraid.*
She stared. What she made of me is wild surmise.
What I made of her is churned with ambivalence.
Still, we looked and that looking was equal.

You know what happened next. I crossed
the electric boundary that she'd set me
and she quit. Not rapidly; pensively; a creature
mindful of the deep strangenesses of the world.
Her hesitation gave me hope. I followed,
quietly, to the top of the rise where the Barrens
stretched out with dissolving invariance.
Already she was submerged, her head
poking from a low thicket of spruce.
I was confined to these shallows; could not
pursue further. I bade her well and withdrew.

Then anticipated, dissuaded, shock: what
has been called *the famous caribou vacillation …
that one more look back at what had scared them.*
Vacillation to match my own. I was crossing
the shale when I checked. She was swinging
down the slope towards me, big easy strides,
nose lifted and eager. The mystery of forgiveness
is not sweeter. I would have come furred
and graceful as her calf for her to claim me.
It could not be. She had stopped, turned oblique.
To break the tension, that hard measure
of our separateness, I stepped out to her.

She retreated. This time the Barrens
would keep her. Sunlight blanched my body back.
I pawed the shale with my boot. Now
the car, the road's thread, could reel me in.

Cape St. Mary's

1

A July day at Cape St Mary's: the fog,
sucked back to its lair, leaves a vague bluff
to smear the horizon, but the afternoon
is stretched across a lazurite ocean
backgrounded by the almost sheer fall
of sky. Under the sun's spotlight, a naked
surface shudders to the cliffs which recede
like a copper banner to margin the Barrens
from the sea. Where you stand, landfall stretches
massive paws to hug a belly of water
that shallows turquoise, aqua, scarved with white.
In the cove's hold, a swirl of insect-like birds,
confetti of gannet and kittiwake;
birdsound brandishes, a ratcheting jabber
of thousands, but below it, seeding
in your ear, soft pulpy deflations,
the mildest explosions; and your gaze floats out
beyond the bay to a vista of sundewed
cerulean where cedars of mist grow
out of gauze. They make sense. You recognise
the plumes of their foliage. You are watching
a forest of whalebreath migrating a blue
savannah. Humpbacks and fin. A great fleet passing.
And you know they are sifting the capelin,
that the silvery harvest is here, spawn
of the Gulf, milt of the current of Labrador.
And look, not all of the whales are sailing by:
some have swung into this harbour, are sliding
on and in, their dark dorsal curves flashing,

their pale patches on belly and fluke
shimmering chlorine-green through the water.
In the pool of the cove, they hang like zeppelins,
great bumble bees glutting the sea's pollen.
Now the chorus of exhalations is like
the whip of metal sheets flapping, a hum
electronically pitched. A single one
is a shed door slamming, gush of thermal breath
from mesenteric depths. The eruptions
make ethereal monuments in a foreign
familiar sphere, this layer they have left
but cannot part from. In and through, birds
flutter like bunting, their shrieking dampened.
Satellite to the display, you watch a marine
Serengeti: the capelin, unseen, but thrashing
like grass; the great herds of beasts underwater;
and, floating on the tide's sloop, blackfly-swarms
of murres and guillemots while, from the heights,
squadrons of gannets strafe to the deep.
Such diverse populations. Such bewildering
numbers. You are utterly irrelevant.
You collapse on the turf to breathe.

2

The herring gulls distract. They stand like courtiers
primed to your movements: jealous; opportunist.
Their stare whets the sound rolling over the headland,
urging you rise and track that harsh babble, which grows
as you climb and follow across rough sheep-cropped
herbage that edges the tundral Barrens. From the air
some gulls keep with you, but now, as you near
the top, they yield to gannets, a grander escort
with their black isosceles of wingtip,
their symmetry of heron-bill, hypodermic tail.
An acid tang of guano scours your pharynx,
flavours the gathering noise, which like the roar
of the crowd at the crucial moment, breaks
as you crest the rise. Land slips away, an open palm;
and there between thick splayed digits, the stack
of Bird Rock. Jostling gannets make a ragged
icefloe on top. The flanking cliffs are spattered
with terraced thousands. Overhead, white
purity of seabird is like a call to clean living, to pare
to essentials, the streamline of *eat; reproduce.*
Here, where land gives out is a tenemented
township of believers: gulls, gannets, kittiwakes;
murres, guillemots, razorbills. A steaming metropolis.
The air holds a chaos of traffic, wheeling, milling,
to confuse all sight. The cacophony routs all thought.
You go to the edge. Bird Rock is just a leap away.

3

The gannets fester with Grecian elegance
on their crude patio. Their buff of nape
and crown glows like a halo against white.
Above a broadsword of bill, eyes are glaucous,
rheumy, the eyes of old men, goggled like First War
pilots. Long shoulders, deep elbows, slope
to black tips crossed over the pointed tail.
Those standing show huge paddles of feet,
burgundy-black webs with rubber-clean
silver-blue piping that runs from the shin
over each toe. Their concerted voices
have the rhythm of corncrakes on speed.
Oh, they are active, they are social, they are
amassed. They pulverise, gather up, sweep
you with them so you bank in and down,
a parent returning to the nest with beakful
of grass or cropful of fish, gliding on albatross
wings, head tilted as your bill points your place,
feet lowered as you hang, flapping, now you're
down, the neighbours are uproarious, but your mate,
your image, is fervent with greeting. You mirror
with preening, bill-clashing, both re-staking
this rough nest, rock slab, partnership, for this
purpose: your frousled young, a caribou-grey
sack of fluff with a swarthy mask and spikish snout.
Once it was trussed in sleep; or, if awake, muzzy
with heat, gargling a pelican throat in the sun.
Now it is frantic, climbing for attention. You turn
to vomit in its maw, then back to your mate
to stroke, to nibble, to fence; to open your wings
as banners, shields, while you squawk and threaten
the neighbours who dare to hunch, to shift,

to be there. But, slowly, calm ripples back
to the eye of the storm; you may even doze,
breast and belly shading your child, your neck
swivelled, slack, so your chin rests on your mantle
and your bill, as it tracks the spine, is scabbarded
by folded wings. And now your mate rises,
swings out to where shoals river the surface,
where the purpose of the body is to circle,
focus, flatten shoulders, close like scissors,
become a spear that plunges, vanishes.

4

You're back on the edge overlooking Bird Rock,
giddy on your human hind legs that feel
powerful enough to make the leap; still caught
in the seethe of brilliance, stridence, but senses, brain,
begin to accommodate. Your gaze is loosed
along the stadium of cliffs; to leisure on serried
ranks of murres veining the strata velvet-brown.
Distinct as beads in a braid, razorbills lift
chisel-nosed heads, hint at an old dark ghost
of these waters. Through gannet factory-noise, a shrill
chatter of kittiwake. Over the edge, where saturated
air is like a membrane enveloping the sharp juts,
their speckled chicks in singles or twos crevice
under a parent's smooth breast. These
are a better class of gull, snowdrop-delicate,
understated, with mantle a cool burnish
of silver, legs a decorous polish of black.
Each solitary brooder splashes the scarp,
an avian anchorite in private contemplation.
You ponder them from your own high perch:
how slight is safety. Yet flight, isolation,
have made a community out of this maelstrom
of species. Each form is a tribal variance.
They encounter each other as equals: any one
a chance; any body a means; to hold
a niche; to further the alchemy of flesh.

5

The sun is greying behind a curtain of vagueness.
Light loses its sharp edge. Like advance
of dusk, slow irresistible clouds are massing,
dissolving everything into their tissue.
Close your eyes. Let yourself soar like a raven.
be the red kite that specked. See the frenzied
colonies, the ribbon of cliffs. Hear the slushy
coughs that spray a fumy surface. Now bank
from the coast to a denser ocean where shoals
of caribou drift through tuckamore. Last view:
a grandstand of pleistocene freshness
where land symmetries the sea's vastness.

Your eyes open to a dew-degged floor
of heather and bracken: you're cloistered
in a tent of gauze. Defined only by the ensign
of wingtip, gannets slip ghostly
in and out of mist: legend's emissaries
in retreat; for the city of birds
is illusory; their voices a mockery.

First Day in Cape Breton

That first day, on our way to Cape North:
the highlands rising like giant loaves;
the tangled jarring release of wilderness.
We soared and swooped the highway's undulations
through bewilderingly boundless forest.
Beyond, the Atlantic floored us, a diamantéd
cobalt, tempting us forward. At McKenzie,
a cluster of vehicles, jeeps, campers, cars,
their occupants spilling onto the road, gawking
with technified eyes into the sprucedepths.
You ask if we should stop but we've been
travelling all day. We need to reach our rest.
As I pull round, I see him, driver's side,
striding along a gully, this lanky
enormity eluding his pursuers
right across from where they peer and probe.

Jesus, get the camera, I blurt and you
dive, obedient. I stab the button
for the window, slide the glass all the way
down. He's really there, our first moose, as real
as any cow in a field, those towering legs
bearing his immense earth-brown bulk
from us. I slow the car to match him, one
hand on the wheel, one juggling the camera,
while he refuses to break dignity
with a run, but inclines his bulbous chalice
of velveted antler away, assesses
the trees for a break in their screen.
As I struggle to trap the alien
mountainous slope of his back in the lens,
I hear you mutter: *Jeepers look behind.*

I glance in the mirror to see we've been spotted:
a headlighted cavalcade looms
after us. From the other direction
two more cars appear, slow and pull in, their
drivers jumping manly onto the road.
At that, the moose climbs up the ditch, presses
through a gap, pushes into the ragged
curtain of spruce. Now others have caught us.
A swarm of tourists skelters across our view,
squawking and snapping. A shadow of moose
stares back from his native cover.

The first man out of the car opposite
approaches my window, his face transfigured.
Where is he? I point to the curious
hulking form, its lowered head juking
under the branches. The man straightens to scan,
then gasp and click. More of the crowd notice
the animal which turns to lumber and
crash his escape through the densely packed trees.
The people sigh. The man looks back to me,
his face rueful and wondering. His own
silence is all I can answer with. When
he looks away, I glance at you. You nod.
I turn back to the wheel and ease my foot
from the brake. We are the first to move off.

The Black Princes

The black princes rise with dusk;
they flower from the leaves of fern
with the sedimentation
of light. They appear

as congealing eddies
of air's semifluid allotrope
or perhaps they're crepuscular
diffusions from imagination's

dark soil. Twilight has pooled
in the clearing, its hoar breathing
off scrub, through slashes of spruce
corpses, the shimmering birches.

An arras of pine bristles
like iron filings electrified
at the brush of a magnet.
Crackle. The darkness shifts,

shapes to bulky rakish creatures:
four moose, all male, are printed
on the bluish mist. They have grown
out of bracken, their legs,

tall as stamens, their full heads
blossoming from the cups
of their bodies. The lobes
of their spread antlers

are gentled by velvet to the soft
contours of ripening fruit. Two
animals are in the centre,
two at opposite sides

of the clearing. They pause.
All heads turn watchfully.
The silence convinces.
They relax, return to browsing

among the ghostly palisades.
Their heads are plunged. Fronds
swish and crack as they tear.
Antlers stir the vegetation.

A small flotilla of moose
is sailing the gauze of dusk
as, from the camber of Earth,
darkness creeps up to stain

the chromatogram of sky.
Foreground shapes become flatter.
In the wings they've dissolved
in the trees. Night thickens

to cloak the black princes,
to leave them condensed as dark
within dark, umbral flickerings
below the depths of mind.

Not Alone

Where the point shrugs
into the Gulf of St Lawrence,

land slips along its last limb
with the gathered folds of a shawl.

The sun's disc burns a thin
meniscus into the horizon's
fat line of navy felt-tip:
an origin, a blazon,
that throws off light
as a scalloped crystalline highway
across water's granite-blue corrugations.

Over the headland's spine
the moon rears to chase her brighter
kin across the arc of sky. Her jaundiced
pockmarked face glowers.

Dark corrals the sky.
The first stars prick its hide

while the sun slips
dragging its cloak
over the ocean's sill.

Dusk precipitates
as a mythical beast:
a chimera with a trollish head,
bovine flanks, folding rod legs.

Yet grace flows in her bulk.

She stops. She has seen you.
Her face averts so just one eye
meets your two. Her ears are forward,
like a horse's, longer. She swings
her head to nuzzle the bracken: a pretence.
Her eyes, both now in the full vase
of her face, glance off yours; but
though alert to you, she comes on.
Your body lightens: you are harmless
or relatively. As she parallels, her ears
flatten and she dips a namaste into a slow
trot, with capacious cycling on sticks
of cannonbones giving the promise,
the power, of flight.

She heads to the point, climbing to overtake you.

She reaches the edge.

She overlooks the Gulf.

She stares down the train of sunset.

The bravery of her undeflectedness;
the uselessness of her purpose.

You follow her gaze,

let your eyes also
feast on beauty;

let your spirit
float up on it.

Finally
you turn;
you enter the veil of dusk

leaving the moose
standing on bare rock

her focus still the sea.

Black Wolf

Real this time. Not
myth-broil, story-weave,
to thicken the pearl of imagination,
make the personal fabulous,
survivable; but bought
with common currencies—
work, time, technology—
distilled to a series of steps:
go to Minnesota; get in a Cessna;
follow the clicks of a radio-collar.

Still, the dark wolf of the mind
is less a surprise
than the wolf of the North Woods.

As the aircraft roars to search height,
terrain becomes a mange of shadow
and snow, thick pelt of spruce, fir,
stippling to bristles of aspen and birch
that bald to the clean-edged blankness
of snow-smothered frozen lake.
Under the plane's wings, flat
antlers of antennae listen for signals
from the Moose Lake pack.

This high, trails are broken capillaries
fretting the lakes' white faces: furrows,
skims, that mark how an animal ploughed
or leaped through chest-deep snow. Once,
a tiny silhouette: a white-tailed deer
like a decoration stencilled on seasonal icing.

Approaching the recognised territory of known
wolves, but miles from where telemetry
will translate sound into sight, the voice
of the pilot, a casual shout, *oh there's one,*
and the plane banks giddyingly
to slide the wolf into view.

Call it coincidence, call it
what you will. The mind closes,
hisses, that what it conjured
and what's out there
don't converge like this;

the world is not made
to give signs and wonders;
has its own laws, its own
necessary evolvings.

It is not there to provide personal comfort.

And then it does.

So you made it to wolf country.
You were promised a sighting.
Now there's your black wolf,
uncollared, on an open plain
of lake. Your retinas burn
as sun switches on the snow.
This is not the same. The animal
is slightly ludicrous as it leaps, furious,
rump swivelling in a push for altitude,
head agitated to see off this infernal
noisy bird that holds you in its bowels.

Which is the true wolf? The one
you made up? Or this large wild dog
dancing in vigorous useless challenge?

The pilot pulls away, flies on to the named
numbered tracked pack we've come to see.
The wolves are bedded, curled like walnuts.

On the sickening return, your eyes cast
for where a snow-bruise breaks a long
thread between the cover of trees;

where the song of the mind was greeted
by the dark flesh of the world.

The Return of the Wolf

A rumour says
they're returning wolves to Yellowstone;
they're talking of a Rhum release.
It'll never come off, of course.
We've tamed the land
and tamed ourselves.
We've no space left
for howling at the moon
or roving through midnight forests.

Our very marrow has absorbed
the tales of Red Riding Hood,
the three little pigs,
the gleaming eyes,
the bared fangs
that lurk
beyond the firelight.

Only within
the halo of its rim
can we see,
can we tell,
are we warm and safe
in the comfort of our knowledge,
in the vision of our understanding,
in the insurance of our control.
In our enlightenment
that blitzes, sears, sanitises,
we automate on,
numb to that absence
we've turned our faces from.

Pining,
we cast about
to sniff it out
but with senses dulled
and bodies heavy, it's
like trying to snare a shadow.
The lore's forgotten.
The trail's nearly dead.
It must be an illusion, a fantasy,
to seduce us from safety.

We shake ourselves, snap
out of it and instead
watch the spellbound
who can't deny the yearning,
who're tempted into the chasm
where they dance
wantonly;
and we sigh
with satisfaction and relief
at our close shave.

We settle and swallow,
follow the rules
that others flaunt
while we blister.
We bide our time,
wait our turn,
allow the ache
under sullen compliance
to fester.

When protest spurts
it leaves us burned
and running for cover
where we're sucked further
into the hollow of our
promise, weeping,
the bigger fools
for believing.

*Don't look
at the sand leaching.
Accept the madness:
strive, earn, achieve;
flaunt the addiction that fuels
our bulimic consumption and makes
us Prime Mover in this shallow
self-contained sphere. Spurn
the voices from the margins.
Bite the big apple and buy
the story for we've smothered
the howl so successfully
that its whimpering echo
sounds laughably strange;*

and we shudder as we look
over our shoulder, listen
over the wail of alarms,
through walls, doors, double glazing
for the baying for our blood
from which we know
no government,

no policy,
no forces,
nobody, nothing,
can save us.

Save us
from the hulk
on the horizon
of our consciousness.

Enclose us
in capsules
so we forget
all that sustains us.

Keep us as we speed
down the road to disaster
from the awareness
that we can't stop

poisoning ourselves
with endless activity
while just behind us
our children choke.

Help us to hurtle on
even though haunted
by the taste of the fumes
in the roofs of our mouths.

May every diffracted
inflation of sunset
mesmerise, hypnotise,

so we close our eyes
to the sludge-scourge wreathing
the wake of each wave.

We flinch from a glimpse
of that stalking shadow
that once upon a time
we were to leave behind.
Off guard, we feel it
at our heels snapping
but we'll not be caught crying
till there's nothing left to lose.

Atishoo,
atishoo,
we'll all
fall
down.

Down, down, deep deep down;
down in the forest of being.
Light slides, diffuses, fades;
the body scrabbles and tears
until panic condenses in the dim
cool deep enveloping dark.

Uncertain calmness; pagan
stillness; some fleeting awareness
of darts, draughts, the twirling
tenderness of tendrils tangling.

Drift and dance,
sway and swoon
and slip deep down
to the bottom, the core,
the kernel, the hub, to the dark
heart, the rub, nub and
nothing.
        Nothing
but the cavern inside –
a rush into space—such
amplifying space that all
the stars, life itself,
could never fill it.

Then:
scurrying, rustling,
the foliage parting;
the blinking, trilling, surging, singing;
the breath intaken, the chest expanding,
the being partaken, that being enough;
the gentle afterswell, the ripple
in every cell, the beginning again,
more than enough.

Only ever
the evocation
to echo
to sound the deep well
now and forever
to the last breath
and final burning
while still believing
in the aftercharge to eddy
the vacuum and oblivion.

We
we were
we were all
all of us
each one
will be here.
And here is enough.

But who is here now
to cry for the wolf's return?
Who will weep
for the waste and the wreckage
and the blundering blind banality
that we stripped, straightened,
hewed, hoed and heaped
from the dark and the deep,
the wanton and the wild?

It is never enough
for we are always afraid,
howling in triumph and despair.
We are all dying here. We always were
even as we grip our future,
the straight and narrow,
that holds us safe and single-minded
but leaves us stranded.

We're unable
to disentangle
from the threads
that bind us all.

The wolf lives
ignorant of our false
dichotomies, our hubris
and desperation
that's reflected
in the violence we project,
the evil and calumny
we heap, onto her fierce
and gentle head;
but she knows
she cannot survive
in our creation
as we slowly realise
that neither can we.

PRAYER FOR THE WOLF'S RETURN

May her winter-breath bless us.
May her tundral spaces sing to us.
May her lunar chorus speak to us
of the need for kinship, worship
and communion with the dark.

May we be as audacious in our living,
as tenacious in our suffering,
as resolute in our accepting
of the cool indifference
to which everything is subject
and through which everything may thrive.

May we hasten to recognise
our sister in spirit,
our brother in blood,
and our own inevitable belonging
in this sacred
only world.

Afterwards

When it is over
I will come home
to moonrise-yellow tundral bleakness,
the bog-brownness glowing
with halogenic infusion,
the shadows crisp,
the woad-black sky
brightening around the well of the moon,
the skin of the birches
ghostly under their dappled capes
and, far off, the inky pines
huddling their cavernous shelter.
I will stand in my openness,
quivering. Across the distance
I will hear them, their deep-timbred
ululations, their quavering soughs.
I will siren them with all the pathos
of my long exile. I will listen
to their answering silence
before they clamour their greeting
with notes of disbelieving joy.
Then I will watch them bead and bob
over the lip of the nearest horizon.
I will wait for them, held
by my breath as it's yanked
by the clench, the surge,
of my heart. Against the dark
cloak of the hill I will track
their rapid time-spinning approach:

the rippling undulations of their strong backs
as they lope unswervingly; the rhythmic
flounce of plumed tails; the missile-steady
poise of fixed heads, the ears forward;
and, nearer, the warm ribbons of tongue,
the amber of their gladdening eyes.
Now they tuck their heads, fold
their ears and crinkle muzzles,
showing the beautiful solid convexity
of nape, the lune-rimed fur.
As they lollop these last
strides, puppyish and playful,
they make adolescents of us all.
I lunge and we collide, chest
to chest, jowl to jowl, black lips
drawn back to whine our pleasure
and tongue the roofs of each other's
mouths, taste the other's sweet
returning flesh. We yip and yowl,
squirm our bodies into a wreath
of greeting, then unravel
to stream across the unfolding
tundra, the hunt only just begun.

NOTES

'Unveiled', p. 18:
George Stubbs' (1724–1806) many images of horses includes a series known as the Rockingham portraits painted on a plain background. This poem is based on *Mares and Foals* (1762).

Robin Blake is an art critic and author of *Stubbs and the Wide Creation* (2005). The term 'equine nudes' is taken from his essay 'A Different Form of Art' published in *Stubbs and the Horse* which coincided with the Stubbs travelling exhibition of 2005.

'Sperrins Autumn', p. 41:
The Amethyst Deceiver, *Laccaria amethystina,* is a small mushroom of distinct hue; more precisely, a mychorrhizal fungus of northern temperate forest, particularly beech woods.

'Avalon', p. 62:
The title refers to the Avalon Peninsula of south-eastern Newfoundland.

'Encounter', p. 68:
The quoted phrase is taken from Lois Crisler's *Arctic Wild.*

'The Return of the Wolf', p. 90:
This poem was inspired by the news in 1995 that the US Fish and Wildlife Service was re-introducing wolves to Yellowstone National Park, reversing the 1926 extirpation of the species there.

Printed in the United Kingdom
by Lightning Source UK Ltd.
131410UK00001B/247-489/P